629: The Prophet sends letters and couriers to the kings of Persia, Yemen and Ethiopia, and to the Emperor Heraclius, to bring to them the message of Islam.

631: Islam is accepted by many Arabian tribes.

630: January (*20 Ramadan, AH 8*): Makkah surrenders without a fight. The Prophet forgives his Makkan opponents. The idols are all taken away from the Kabah and all of the people there accept Islam.

622: A plot is hatched in Makkah to kill the Prophet Muhammad. To save his life, the Prophet goes away to Madinah, which marks the beginning of the Islamic calender known as Hijrah. The Prophet receives a warm welcome from the people of Madinah. Most of his followers leave Makkah for Madinah.

605: The Prophet Muhammad helps to rebuild the Kabah.

Madinah

Arabia

616: Persecution increases. The Prophet, his family and followers are boycotted by Makkans.

594: Khadijah, a widow and merchant, employs the Prophet Muhammad to sell her goods. He travels to Syria taking her goods to trade there.

Sea

Makkah

595: The Prophet Muhammad marries Khadijah. They have four daughters and two sons. Sadly, both sons die very young.

ophet
akkah. His
al-Muttalib,
his birth.

610: Beginning of the Prophet's mission. The Angel Gabriel reveals the first few verses of the Quran to him while he is thinking about God in the Cave of Hira near Makkah. Khadijah, Ali, Abu Bakr and Zayd become the first Muslims.

mad's mother, takes
Makkah, Aminah dies.
his grandfather, Abd
Abu Talib)

613: The Prophet starts preaching Islam to the people of Makkah. Not many respond to his call. Most Makkans oppose him, treating him and his followers with scorn and cruelty.

ajj
deliver

sest

Arabian Gulf

Ethiopia

620: The Prophet goes to Taif to seek help, but the people of the city turn him away, urging street children to pelt him with stones. He is wounded all over his body and blood collects in his shoes.

Tell Me About
THE PROPHET
MUHAMMAD ﷺ

SANIYASNAIN KHAN

Goodword
B·O·O·K·S

First published 2000
© Goodword Books, 2000

Goodword Press
The Islamic Centre, Al-Risala
1, Nizamuddin West Market
New Delhi, 110 013
Tel. (9111) 4626666, 4625454
Fax (9111) 4697333, 4647980
e-mail: skhan@vsnl.com

Photographic Credits:
Peter Sanders, cover (centre, top right, bottom left,
bottom right), first end pages (left), 1,2 (top), 3 (top right,
bottom), 5,7,8,16,19,27,30,31,
32,35,37,38,40,43,45,49,55, last end pages, back
cover (top right, bottom left);
Mohamed Amin, end pages (bottom
right), 47; **Ruqaiyyah Waris Maqsood,**
first end pages (top right); **Madan
Mehta,** 10; **Aramco World,** first end
pages (middle right); **Goodword
Press,**
cover (top left), 2 (bottom), 29.

Thanks are due to Anna Khanna,
Susan Brady Maitra and
Farida Khanam for their immense
help in making this book possible.

Illustrations: K.M. Ravindran

Printed and bound in India

CONTENTS

1. Birth of the Prophet

The Prophet Muhammad ﷺ was born in 570 A.D., in the land of Arabia. Much of Arabia is desert—vast, silent, barren regions where the stars loom large at night and where people depend for their survival upon shade, water and each other's goodwill. There were three major towns, Yathrib, a large oasis now called Madinah, Taif, a cool refuge in the mountains famous for its grapes and Makkah which by contrast, lay in a barren valley. It was in Makkah that the Prophet first saw the light of day. Now famous as the birthplace of the Prophet Muhammad and the focal point of the Hajj pilgrimage, Makkah was important in those days because it was at the junction of many trading routes. It was even more important as the home of the Kabah, where people came from far and wide to worship. The original Kabah was built by the Prophets Ibrahim and Ismail, whose lives were particularly devoted to God.

As ill luck would have it, the Prophet Muhammad's father, Abdullah, died two months before his birth, and his mother, Aminah, was naturally very sad. But still, she felt strong and well as she waited for her baby to be born. When he came into the world, Aminah sent word to her father-in-law, Abd al-Muttalib, who was sitting near the Kabah as he always did.

Abd al-Muttalib was the head of the Quraysh tribe, guardian of the Kabah and protector of the pilgrims who visited this holy

place. He was respected and admired by all. But he was not like the other Arabs who had drifted away from the teachings of the Prophet Ibrahim (Abraham) and had begun again to worship idols. He was one of the *hanifs*, or pious people, who believed in Allah, the one true God, with all his heart.

He was happy to hear the news of the birth and began to think of a name for the baby boy. Finally, he decided upon Muhammad, an unusual name that means "often praised", or "worthy of praise".

Some time before his birth, believers had prayed for a prophet to come, and there had been signs that Allah had heard their prayers. Jewish scriptures told of a prophet that was to come. On the night of the Prophet's birth a learned Jew in Yathrib saw a brilliant star he had never seen before. He called people together around him and, pointing to the star, told them that a Prophet must have been born. Word spread quickly.

The original Kabah was built by the Prophets Ibrahim and Ismail, whose lives were entirely devoted to God. But over the centuries people began to drift away from the One God and set up idols there to many other gods. In the days of the Prophet Muhammad, the Kabah was surrounded by 360 altars, statues and cult objects of these various deities. The most important tribe living in and around Makkah was the Quraysh. They were merchants who had control of both the Kabah and Makkah s water supply. They profited greatly from giving protection to and catering for the needs of the vast numbers of traders, who came from far and wide to buy and sell, and the thousands of pilgrims from many different countries. It was into this tribe that the Prophet Muhammad was born.

An Example to All Human Beings

God sends prophets into the world to show us how to live. That is why God sent the Prophet Muhammad into the world also. But He did not want him to live like a hermit, to give up the world and go and live by himself in a mountain cave, or in a forest. Granted, it is much easier to lead a pure life and to think about the Almighty when you are not troubled by worldly matters and you are away from people and temptations. But because God wanted the Prophet to be a shining example to humanity, He destined him to live amongst other human beings, like any other ordinary man — to have a family, to work for his living and to have his share of troubles, joys and sorrows.

2. Nursed in the Desert

The Prophet's Advice to His Daughter

'Ali, the son of Abu Talib, related how Fatimah, his wife and also daughter of the Prophet Muhammad, had to do all the housework herself. Her hands used to become blistered from working a millstone, her clothes became dirty from sweeping the floor, and she had a mark on her neck from having to bring water from outside in a large leather bag. On one occasion when the Prophet had many servants come to him, 'Ali suggested to Fatimah that she go and request her father to give her one of them. But there were many people gathered at his house, so she returned home without meeting him. The next day the Prophet came to the house of 'Ali and Fatimah and asked what she had wanted to discuss, but Fatimah remained silent. Then 'Ali told the Prophet the whole story. The Prophet did not, however, say yes to their request. "Fear God," he said, "and fulfil your duty to the Lord. Continue to do your housework and, when you go to bed at night, glorify Allah 33 times, praise Him the same number of times and exalt him 34 times. That makes 100 times altogether. That will do you more good than a servant will." *(Al-Targheeb wa al-Tarheeb)*

It was the custom in those days, in Makkah, for mothers to send their babies into the desert to be nursed by paid foster mothers from among the people who tended sheep. The weather in the desert, away from the city, was considered more healthy. Aminah, too, did this, and so the little Muhammad ﷺ spent the first years of his life with a woman named Halimah and her family of the Banu Sa'd tribe.

Halimah worried that she would not be able to care properly for the baby Muhammad ﷺ. They were very poor, and because of the previous year's famine, she had hardly enough milk to feed her own baby. But

as soon as she began nursing Muhammad ﷺ, her milk increased. After they got back home, many things began to change for the better. The land became green, and the date palms grew heavy with fruit. Dates were one of the family's main foods. The sheep and camels regained their health. Halimah and her husband knew that these blessings were because of the baby Muhammad ﷺ.

Muhammad ﷺ grew well during his stay with Halimah and her family. He played with her children, and together they would take the sheep to graze. When Muhammad ﷺ returned to Aminah, he was a strong and healthy three year old.

Good Family Ties

The Prophet revered parents. He would say: "Paradise lies at the feet of mothers," and "God's pleasure is in the father's pleasure; and God's displeasure is in the father's displeasure." Those, he believed, who served their parents well, were deserving of Paradise. A man once asked the Prophet, "Who rightfully deserves the best treatment from me?" "Your mother," said the Prophet. Then the man said, "Who comes next?" "Your mother," said the Prophet. "Who is after that?" asked the man, "Your mother," was the Prophet's answer. "Who comes next?" insisted the man again. "Your father," said the noble Prophet.

The Prophet gave great importance to family ties. He said, "The best man is he who is best to his wife."

A desert outside Makkah. It was one such area where the Prophet Muhammad spent his early days.
▼

3. A Visit to Yathrib

When Muhammad ﷺ was six, Aminah decided to take him with her to visit his uncles in Yathrib. Yathrib (now known as Madinah) was situated in the midst of volcanic hills in the Hijaz region of western Saudi Arabia about 100 miles (160 km) inland from the Red Sea. In its early days, it was an oasis famed for the dates from its palm groves.

It was a long journey by caravan, but young Muhammad ﷺ enjoyed meeting his cousins, playing with them and learning to swim. Muhammad ﷺ and Aminah enjoyed the pleasant climate and the company of their relatives for a month. But, tragically, on the journey back to Makkah, Aminah fell ill and died. Little Muhammad returned home with Aminah's maid, Barakah.

Muhammad's grandfather adopted him and took care of him. Abd al-Muttalib loved Muhammad ﷺ dearly, and was convinced that he was destined for greatness. Muhammad ﷺ sat by Abd al-Muttalib's side near the Kabah during

◄ A minaret of an old mosque in Madinah surrounded by green palm trees.

all his consultations, and when
Abd al-Muttalib fell sick two years
later, Muhammad ﷺ attended to
him faithfully. When his grandfather
died, Muhammad ﷺ was adopted by his
uncle, Abu Talib. Muhammad ﷺ became part
of Abu Talib's large family right
away, and was his favourite.

4. A Thoughtful Boy

We also learn from the stories of his life that Muhammad ﷺ was a very thoughtful boy. He took good care of his family's sheep, and played with the other children. But he also spent much time alone, wondering about the mysteries of nature. He thought about the people around him, how they lived and how they behaved. Even when he was a very little boy, Halimah said that she often found him sitting by himself.

In the creation of the heavens and the earth, and in the alternation of night and day, there are signs for men of sense; those that remember God when standing, sitting, and lying down, and reflect upon the creation of the heavens and the earth.

—Surah Āl-'Imran, 3:190-191

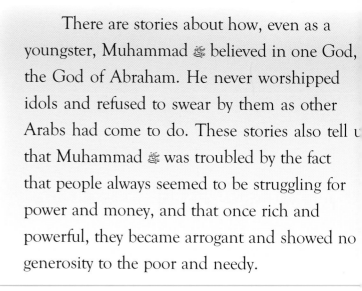

There are stories about how, even as a youngster, Muhammad ﷺ believed in one God, the God of Abraham. He never worshipped idols and refused to swear by them as other Arabs had come to do. These stories also tell u that Muhammad ﷺ was troubled by the fact that people always seemed to be struggling for power and money, and that once rich and powerful, they became arrogant and showed no generosity to the poor and needy.

Knowledge as Your Friend

"Acquire knowledge!" the Prophet Muhammad ﷺ used to tell his followers. "Seeking knowledge is the duty of every Muslim. It will enable you to be your own friend in the desert, it will be your mainstay in solitude, your companion in loneliness, your guide to happiness, your sustainer in misery, your adornment when you are amongst people and your arrow against your enemies. Whoever goes out in search of knowledge is on the path of Allah until returning."

Another of the Prophet's sayings was that if anyone went on his way in search of knowledge, God would make it easy for him to find the way to Paradise.

THE FAITHFUL TRUSTEE

We do not know exactly what Muhammad ﷺ looked like, but his cousin, 'Ali ibn Abi Talib, has given us some idea. 'Ali said Muhammad ﷺ was of medium height, and broad-shouldered, and had curly hair and a thick beard. His walk conveyed strength and resolution: he walked softly but firmly, with large swift strides, and bent slightly forward. Some say the ground seemed to roll itself up for him, and his disciples had to work hard to keep up with him even when the Prophet walked at a leisurely pace.

The Prophet's skin was tawny and his eyes shown light brown from under bushy eyebrows. The Prophet's eyes did not wander around, looking at this and that. They were usually downcast. But when he did look up at something he would look straight into it.

By the time he was 25 years old, Muhammad ﷺ had a reputation for honesty. He was known among the Quraysh as the bravest and most gentlemanly person. He was a good neighbour, tolerant and always truthful. He always kept aloof from quarrels and quibbles, and never used foul language or abuse. 'Ali ibn Abi Talib once said, "All who came close to him grew to love him."

5. Marriage and Friendship

Muhammad's experience of trading, together with his excellent reputation, drew him to the attention of Khadijah, a beautiful and wealthy widow belonging to a family of merchants. Khadijah employed Muhammad ﷺ to take her goods to trade in Syria.

Muhammad ﷺ handled the trading very well, and brought back more profits than Khadijah had ever made before. Also, Khadijah's servant, Maysarah, who accompanied Muhammad ﷺ to Syria, had come to admire and respect him greatly, and gave a glowing report to her mistress about what a superior person Muhammad ﷺ was.

Khadijah wanted to marry Muhammad ﷺ whose refined speech and looks had made such a profound impression upon her. When Khadijah conveyed her willingness to marry him through her friend, Nufaysah, Muhammad ﷺ, having great respect for

Zayd ibn Haritha

Zayd was travelling with his father, Haritha, when their caravan was attacked. He was dragged away to a bazaar and sold there as a slave. The person who bought him, Khadijah, thought he would be useful to her husband, Muhammad ﷺ. But the Prophet did not like the idea of slavery, so when the boy's father Haritha came to Makkah and begged him to give him back, saying that he would pay whatever he wanted, the Prophet told him that he did not want any compensation. If Zayd wanted to go with him, he could take him. Much to Haritha's surprise, Zayd said that he had been shown so much love by the Prophet that he preferred to stay with him. The Prophet Muhammad then took Zayd to the Kabah, and in the presence of Zayd's father and uncle, announced to everyone that this boy was now his son. Haritha and his brother went away happily, knowing that Zayd was in good hands.

Khadijah, happily said yes. The marriage was a joyful one. They were well suited to each other, and were blessed with six children, two boys and four girls. Sadly, however, both sons died at an early age.

Khadijah was not only Muhammad's wife, but also his friend and helper, and, later, first his disciple. When the Quraysh's persecution of the Prophet was at its height, just before Muhammad's decision to leave Makkah, Khadijah died. It was a terrible loss for Muhammad .

In the years after Khadijah's death, Muhammad married other wives. He had only one more child, by the last of these wives, a son named Ibrahim, who also died in infancy.

Speaking the Truth

The Prophet Muhammad once remarked with great wisdom that you should always tell the truth, because that leads to a life of virtue, and that you should stay away from people who tell lies, because that leads to a life of evil. Indeed, the noblest quality in a man or woman is honesty. It shines forth, showing purity of soul. One who tells lies mars his inner self and sinks deeper and deeper into evil. The Prophet observed: "The best utterance to me is that of truth. The trader who is truthful and trustworthy will be raised on Doomsday along with the Prophets." (al-Bukhari)

6. The Pledge: A Leader of Men

Even as a boy, Muhammad ﷺ was concerned about his fellow men. One day a trader from Yemen had his goods stolen by a group of wicked Makkans. The trader called out for help, but no one came forth. So the trader wrote a poem that made fun of the Makkans' bad behaviour, and recited it out loud in public for all to hear. When Zubayr, one of Muhammad's uncles, heard this poem, he felt ashamed. Zubayr called the city elders to a meeting, and an organisation was formed to protect the oppressed people of Makkah. This included foreign visitors as well as the people who had always lived there. Muhammad ﷺ became an enthusiastic member of the group, called Hilf al-Fudul, who pledged themselves to be courteous and considerate towards others, especially those weaker than themselves.

Even many years later, Muhammad ﷺ kept this promise to Hilf al-Fudul, saying: "I am not prepared to break my promise, even against a herd of camels; if somebody should appeal to me even today, by virtue of that pledge, I would hurry to his help."

The Prophet Muhammad's sense of justice, his prompt understanding of problems and his real interest in his fellow men combined to make him a leader. He could always be relied upon to judge fairly and was more and more sought out to help settle disputes. His fame got a mighty boost by an incident that took place when Muhammad ﷺ was not more than 35 years old.

The Kabah caught fire and burned to the ground. All the tribes of Makkah took part in repairing it and building it up again, but when it was time to put back the sacred Black Stone first laid by

STRENGTH OF CHARACTER

There was an old Makkan woman who hated the Prophet. Every morning when he passed by her house, she would empty a basket of rubbish on his head from the upper story of her house. He never grumbled or said anything to her. One day she was and in bed when he passed that way. Surprised that no rubbish had been emptied on his head, he thought, "She must be ill," and went upstairs to enquire how she was. The woman was very frightened. She thought he had come to quarrel with her. When he said he had come to enquire after her health, she began to cry. "What a good man you are," she sobbed. "I ill-treat you and you enquire after my health. Teach me your religion. Teach me your way of life." This shows what strength of character, what patience and tolerance the Prophet had in refusing to be provoked, and in his kindness and generosity towards one who wished him ill.

the Prophet Abraham, there was a crisis. Each of the four leading families of Makkah claimed that they alone should have that honour. Finally, it was agreed that the first man to enter the courtyard of the Kabah would settle the issue. That man was Muhammad ﷺ.

It seemed like a problem which could not be solved, but Muhammad ﷺ had a simple idea that saved the honour of everyone concerned. He spread out a white sheet on the ground and placed the sacred stone at its center. Then he instructed the elders of each clan to lift a corner of the sheet and carry the stone to its site. Then Muhammad ﷺ, the peacemaker, fixed the stone in its place with his own hands.

The Black Stone

At the eastern corner of the Kabah, about 5 feet above the ground, there is an oval black stone of about 18 cm in diameter fixed in the wall.

This stone was originally set there by the Prophet Ibrahim ﷺ to mark the spot from which to begin the *tawaf* of the Kabah. Now this is the only relic of the original building.

7. The Search for Truth

The Prophet Muhammad's marriage with Khadijah gave him every opportunity to lead a comfortable life as a wealthy and respected noble of Makkah. And, indeed, for a few years Muhammad ﷺ did lead a calm and quiet life as a merchant. But he soon gave up all worldly activity and set himself to searching for the truth.

Instead of meeting people all the time in their homes and at gatherings, and trying to gain for himself a position among the nobles of Makkah, Muhammad ﷺ would wander into the barren hills of the desert. He would

◄

The Cave of Hira, where the first revelation of the Quran was made to the Prophet Muhammad. The cave, which is large enough for a man to say his prayers, is situated at the summit of the Jabal an-Nur, or the Mountain of Light, to the north east of Makkah, a few miles away from the city on the road to Mina.

sit for hours and ponder the mysteries of creation. The vast silence of the desert, with endless sand and sky and, at night, equally endless darkness, alive only with the twinkling of millions and millions of tiny stars, seemed to bring one very close to the Creator.

For days, Muhammad ﷺ would often stay alone in the cave of Hira, which was near the top of Jabal al-Nur or the Mountain of Light, three miles from Makkah. He would return home only for more supplies of food and water, and then go back to the solitude of nature to pray and meditate, asking the Maker of the heavens and the earth for answers to the questions that surged in his mind. What is man's true role in life? What does the Lord require of us, as His servants? From where does man come, and where will he go after death?

On the twelfth of February, 610 A.D., Muhammad ﷺ, now forty years of age, went to the Cave of Hira near the top of Mount al-Nur to spend Ramadan, the traditional month of retreat. He was sitting all alone in this cave, when he had an extraordinary experience.

Laws of Islam

Here are some of the laws which the Prophet Muhammad ﷺ taught his followers.

- Control your anger, then forgive your brother. Do you not wish to be forgiven?
- Do not hate each other, envy each other or provoke each other.
- Do not spy on each other, or betray each other's trust.
- Do not speak ill of your friend behind his back.
- Give the labourer his wages before his sweat dries.
- Do not drink alcohol, and do not gamble—it opens the door to the devil.
- Do not steal the property of another.
- Do not cheat each other.
- Do not charge interest on money loaned to those who need it.
- Do not take part in corrupt practices or do anything of which you would be ashamed if it became known.
- Do not reveal your friends' weaknesses. Cover up their failings if you wish God to cover up yours.
- Do not pay bribes to get what is not lawfully yours.
- Do not be cruel to animals.
- Gladden the heart of the afflicted, feed the hungry, give comfort to the sorrowful and remove the wrongs of the injured.

8. The Night of Destiny

Suddenly, after many days of meditation, the Archangel Gabriel appeared before Muhammad ﷺ in human form. "Read!" commanded the angel. "I cannot read," Muhammad ﷺ protested. So the angel held Muhammad ﷺ tightly by the shoulders, shook him, and taught him these words:

> Read: In the name of your Lord who created, created man from a clot.
> Read: And your Lord is the Most Generous Who taught by the pen,
> Taught man what he did not know.

These were the first words of the Holy Quran. Muhammad ﷺ felt these lines actually written on his heart. But the experience left him surprised and confused. He even felt he might be falling ill. He rushed back to his wife, Khadijah, who comforted him. She took him to her cousin, Waraqah, who told him that the revelation he had had was from the same source as the messages of Moses and Jesus. Gradually he began to understand—his quest had finally been rewarded. His restless, searching soul had been joined with his Lord. Allah not only gave him guidance, but He also chose Muhammad ﷺ as His Prophet and special Messenger, to bring His word to a world that had gone badly astray. It was a tremendous responsibility. But Muhammad ﷺ, far from becoming vain or proud, remained as good and humble a man as ever. He continued to receive divine revelations from time to time over the next twenty three years, when the Archangel Gabriel would come to him in different forms, sometimes huge and filling the horizon, and sometimes just a pair of eyes watching him. Sometimes he remained invisible. Occasionally only his voice could be heard. Sometimes it was muffled, like a ringing in his head. But the meaning was always clear.

Muhammad ﷺ could neither make the revelations happen, nor stop them. They might happen while he was making a speech, while sitting, while praying, or even while riding his camel. He always knew when they were about to happen, and his Companions could see the change come over him. He would fall silent, and normally lay down covered in his cloak. His face might

become red and he would perspire profusely, even on cold days. His Companions said if you were near him, you could hear something like humming around his face. The experience of the revelations always seemed to make the Prophet Muhammad ﷺ feel close to death, as if he was leaving his body and might never return. "Not once did I receive a revelation without thinking that my soul had been torn away," said the Prophet. At the end of the experience Muhammad ﷺ would return to normal, and recite the new verses of the Quran. His Companions were instructed to record them.

The Cave of Hira at the top of the Mountain of Light near Makkah.

The Quran— A Supreme Miracle

The Prophet Muhammad faced many people in his lifetime who did not believe in him. They challenged him to work a miracle like the Prophet Jesus in order to prove that God had really sent him as His messenger. This he did not do. He retorted that it was quite unnecessary, as the Quran itself was the supreme miracle. If anyone doubted it, let them try to compose ten *surahs* that would bear comparison with it:

"Produce ten invented chapters like it. Call on whom you will among your idols, if what you say be true." (11:12).

He also pointed out that there were obvious signs of God everywhere—in the beauty of nature, in life-giving water, in the growth of crops and in the miracle of birth. The entire universe, in fact, was proof of His existence as the Creator and Sustainer.

Allah's message to His prophets was made directly through the angel Gabriel (Jibril). The Quran is the final revelation, which was made to the Prophet Muhammad. There were two main ways in which the revelations came to him. Sometimes the angel Gabriel would reveal the verses of the Quran as one man to another. This way it was easy. But, at other times, it was like the ringing of a bell piercing his heart and tearing him apart. This method was very hard and painful. The revelation of the Quran started when the Prophet was 40 years old and continued in parts all throughout his life for 23 years. The last revelation of the Quran came only a few months before his death, when the Prophet was 63 years of age.

9. The Messenger of God

These astonishing events were at first difficult for people to understand. They were still living in an age which is now called the "Days of Ignorance." And remember that after the first revelation, the Prophet Muhammad ﷺ himself had been totally shaken by the experience. It had only been very gradually, with Khadijah's help, that he had come to understand and accept what had happened—that he had been chosen by Allah as His messenger to mankind.

Like Khadijah, the Prophet's family and friends realized he was an intelligent, kind and down-to-earth person. The revelations he received were not tinged with selfishness, hatred or ill-will. They were a clear guide to righteousness, and an insight into the kingdom of God. Khadijah was the first to respond to the call of the Prophet. Her cousin, the wise man Waraqah, explained to her that just as Gabriel had come to Moses earlier on Mount Sinai and told him to guide his people, so too would Muhammad ﷺ be the Prophet of his people. But Waraqah also warned that not all

the people would listen to the Prophet, and some would even try to harm him and his followers. Muhammad ﷺ would need great courage and patience, he said. Khadijah understood, and became the strongest help and support to Muhammad ﷺ in the trials that followed.

The next to respond to the Prophet was his cousin, 'Ali. Zayd, his foster son, was the third one. The first convert from outside the family was Abu Bakr, a respected merchant who became the Prophet's closest Companion. At first Muhammad ﷺ taught Khadijah and the small group of friends how to pray, and they would pray together. At a certain point, after the Prophet had been doing this for three years, the angel Gabriel commanded Muhammad ﷺ to speak openly, and he began to hold public meetings. Slowly the message of Allah, the Maker of heaven and earth and all the things in heaven and on earth, began to spread.

The Divine Message

The message the Prophet Muhammad ﷺ brought was not to the liking of many Arabs. He preached that they should worship only one God. He told them they must show proper respect for women and should not lie, or cheat, or take money which rightfully belonged to the poor and to orphans. Nor should they lend money at a high rate of interest. They must stop drinking and gambling and killing for revenge. He impressed upon people that there really was a life after death, and there would come a time of judgement when they would be rewarded or punished according to how they had lived. Had they thought only of money-making and their own comfort and luxury? Or had they given freely to orphans, widows, the sick, the hungry and the needy? Had they bowed humbly to God in worship and prayer? The Prophet Muhammad had to convince everyone that, even if they did not believe in life after death, they would be forced to do so once they experienced it. By that time it would be too late to feel sorry and beg forgiveness for all their bad deeds and all the good things they had omitted to do. Their lives were a test of their ability to do their duty to God and mankind. The most important quality a person could develop in relation to good and evil was *taqwa,* that is, being conscious of God at all times and being careful not to overstep the limits set by Him.

True, Allah was merciful and knew all about everyone and their reasons for behaving the way they did—and if people were truly sorry for their bad thoughts and actions, they would be forgiven. But God was also perfectly just—if people who had passed a lifetime doing bad things were still not sorry about them by the time they died, they would not be forgiven. To forgive them would not be fair, and Allah was always fair.

The Quraysh of Makkah felt particularly threatened. The Prophet's message that there was only one God, and that all men were brothers who served Allah, challenged the way the Quraysh had come to live. They worshipped many different idols, believed in all kinds of magic, fought amongst each other for worldly gain, upheld the code of blood-feud or vengeance, and oppressed and mistreated those who were poorer and weaker than they.

The Prophet's own tribe was in charge of the Kabah with its idols and when they realized that he was trying to stop people from worshipping them, they were furious because they thought their profit was in danger.

10. Justice

Before Islam, the blood feud prevailed: when a member of a group was injured or killed by a person from another group, the first group had the right of vengeance, a tooth for a tooth, a life for a life. But the Quran praised the Muslim who accepted a penalty less severe on the criminal than warranted by his crime, or who forgave altogether. The Quran also decreed that if a believer deliberately killed another, he would be punished in Hell; if accidentally, he would pay blood money.

The Quraysh tried in many ways, including the use of force, to dissuade the Prophet Muhammad ﷺ from his path, and to stop the message from spreading. They were determined to crush the movement at all costs, because they were too proud to admit the error of their ways and change their beliefs and practices.

So the Prophet Muhammad ﷺ

was subjected to every kind of cruelty and insult. Thorns were strewn in his path, stones were thrown at his house, and he was pelted with dirt and rubbish. He was laughed at and ridiculed. Once, when he was praying in the Kabah, a sheet was thrown round his neck and pulled with such force that he fell on his face.

The Prophet Muhammad's Companions, too, faced all kinds of persecution. For example, when Bilal ibn Rabah, a slave, entered the fold of Islam, he was tortured by his master. He was thrown down on the sand under the burning sun, and kept there with a heavy stone on his chest. "*Ahad! Ahad! Ahad!*" (Allah the One, the One, the One) were the only words he uttered. Later Abu Bakr was able to free Bilal.

The Second Pillar of Islam

"Give glory to your Lord before sunrise and before sunset. Praise Him day and night, so that you may find comfort." (The Quran, 20:130)

In Islam, everyone faces God alone, on a one-to-one basis. There is no priest, no special knowledge, no sacrifice or ceremony needed to put one in touch with God. This is why *salah,* or prayer is such an important part of Islam. It is meant to bring people close to Allah, to purify their hearts and bring about moral and spiritual growth.

The performance of *salah*—always done facing the Kabah in Makkah—is based on the way the Prophet himself prayed. In its movements and words, its practice is more like worship than the personal appeals we usually think of as prayer. Each cycle of it is called a *rakah.* Though it is a ritual in form, only the purity of heart and mind, and the humility of the worshipper give it meaning. Some of the words are part of the regular routine, and others are chosen by the individual from the Quran.

One of the most famous prayers of the Prophet is known as the 'Prayer of Light': "O Allah, place light in my heart, light in my sight, light in my hearing, light on my right and on my left, light above me, light below me. O Allah, Who knows the innermost secrets of our hearts, lead me out of the darkness into the Light."

Muslims can pray alone wherever they are at the prayer times, or they can join all the other worshippers who are saying prayers at the mosque. The Friday midday prayer at the mosque is compulsory for all Muslim males to attend. When many people pray together at this time, this is called 'congregational' prayers.

The preparation for prayers is also part of the *salah,* and this is meant to train believers in cleanliness, punctuality and self-discipline, and in having the ability to rise above personal worries or passing fancies. Of first importance is *niyah,* or intention; and this refers to the process of closing one's mind to worldly distractions, cleaning one's body and choosing a clean place to pray. The ritual cleansing, called *wudu,* is done in a quiet and prayerful way.

The Prophet, being a very considerate person, did not want worshippers to suffer any unnecessary hardship while saying their prayers. One day he went into the mosque and saw a rope stretched between two pillars. "What is this rope?" he asked, and was told that it belonged to Zaynab. She clung to it when weakened by fatigue. The Prophet said, "Untie it! Let each of you pray while you have the energy to do so and then sit down when you are tired."

11. A Christian King Helps Out

In 619, five years after the beginning of the revelation of the Quran, a group of the Prophet's Companions, weary of daily torture and hardship, left Makkah on the Prophet's advice to seek shelter in Abyssinia with the Christian ruler, King Negus (Najashi). Under cover of nightfall 16 of them slipped away, to be followed later by another 83 men and women. When the Makkans discovered this, they were enraged, particularly because the children of many leading families were among them. The Quraysh leaders sent two of their cleverest men to persuade King Negus to send the Muslims back. On arrival, they first gave gifts to the King's advisers, saying that some "foolish Makkans" had recently migrated to Abyssinia and that they intended to ask the king for their return. Then they went to the King, and said, "Your Majesty, these people have abandoned the religion of Makkah, but they have not even become Christians like you." The King's advisers promptly urged him to hand them over straight away. But the King, unconvinced, became angry, saying, "No, by

God, they came to me for protection and I will hear what they have to say." The Makkans were dismayed at this, realizing that the King would immediately sense the migrants' sincerity. When the Muslims entered, they did not bow before King Negus and were thereupon rebuked by the advisers. But the Muslims simply said, "We kneel only to Allah." Then King Negus asked them about their religion. The Muslims' spokesman, Ja'far ibn Abi Talib, 'Ali's brother and the Prophet's cousin, said: "O King, we and our ancestors turned away in ignorance from the faith of the Prophet Ibrahim, who with Ismail, built the Kabah and worshipped only Allah. We did quite unspeakable things, worshipping idols, treating our neighbours unfairly, oppressing the weak and so on. This was our life until Allah sent a Messenger from among us, one of our own

Jesus in the Quran

Jesus, one of the great prophets, is frequently mentioned in the Quran. *Surah 19*, which is named after Mary, the mother of Jesus, tells in graphic detail of the miraculous birth of Jesus, and concludes with the pure words of Jesus, which he spoke while he was an infant in the cradle:

I am Allah's servant;
He has given me the Book, and made me a Prophet.
He has made me Blessed, wherever I may be;
and He has commanded me to pray, and to give alms,
so long as I live, and likewise to cherish my mother;
He has not made me arrogant or wicked.
I was blessed the day I was born,
and peace be upon me, the day I die, and the day I am raised up alive!

—*Surah Maryam*, 19:30-32

relatives, known always to have been honest, innocent and faithful. He asked us to worship only Allah, to give up the bad customs of our forefathers, to be truthful and trustworthy, to respect and help our neighbours, to honour our families and look after orphans, and to put an end to misdeeds and fighting. He ordered us to slander neither men nor women. He bade us worship none other than Allah, to pray, to give alms and to fast. We believe in him and follow his lead. The Makkans began to come between us and our religion, so we left our homes and came to you, hoping to find justice." Hearing this, Negus said, "Tell me some of the revelations which your Prophet claims to have received from God." Ja'far then recited some Quranic verses in which Mary, the pure and devoted mother of Jesus, has to face angry and disbelieving family members. She points to the baby Jesus, but they say they cannot speak to a mere baby. Then Jesus himself astonishes them by uttering words of great wisdom. Overwhelmed at this, the King exclaimed: "The messages of Jesus and Muhammad come from the same source!" And drawing a line with his cane on the floor, he said joyfully, "Between your religion and ours there is really no more difference than this line." With that he gave the Muslims his permission to live peacefully in his realm. The clever Makkans were sent home bitterly disappointed.

12. The Year of Sorrow

In the meantime the Quraysh had imposed a social ban on the Prophet Muhammad's family in Makkah. No one was to talk to them or conduct business with them. This ban lasted for three years, and caused the family great suffering. During this period, the Prophet's faithful wife and greatest help, Khadijah, died. Then, Abu Talib, the Prophet's loving uncle and guardian, also died.

These were harsh blows. Abu Talib was a respected elder of the Quraysh. Though not a follower of Islam, he had protected the Prophet against his enemies. It is Arab custom that someone under the protection of another is safe as long as the protector lives. Now, with the death of his uncle, the Prophet ﷺ was without protection. His enemies cheered, and redoubled their brutalities.

In 619 A.D., nine years now after the beginning of the revelation of the Quran, and despairing of his work in Makkah, the Prophet went to Ta'if, a nearby city, to spread his message and seek help. But the people of Ta'if refused to listen to the Prophet. They jeered at him and drove him out of town, setting the street urchins

After being ill-treated by the people of Taif, the Prophet, wounded from head to foot and very downhearted, set out on the return journey. At dusk he took refuge in a vineyard belonging to two brothers, Utbah and Shybah. They took pity on the Prophet and sent their servant Addas with some fresh grapes. Addas told him he was a Christian and hailed from Nineveh in Iraq. So you are from the town of the good Jonah (Yunus), son of Matthew, observed the Prophet. How do you know Jonah? Addas asked him. He was a prophet, and so am I, said the Prophet. On hearing this, Addas bowed before the Prophet, kissing his head, hands and feet.

▼

to pelting him with stones. The Prophet's body was covered with wounds, and he was bleeding from head to toe.

Suddenly, the Archangel Gabriel appeared along with Malak al-Jibal, the Angel of the Mountain. Malak al-Jibal asked if he should crush the people of Ta'if between two mountains. "No," said the noble Prophet, and he raised his hands instead to pray for the people of Ta'if: "Lord, guide them. I am hopeful for their descendants, who will one day serve Your cause." Then he returned to Makkah.

The Mountains of Taif. Somewhere here the angel of the Mountains appeared to the Prophet Muhammad, seeking his permission to crush the people of Taif for their ill-treatment of him. But the Prophet, although in pain and distress, only raised his hands towards the sky and said, No, O my Lord! What is really remarkable is that he began to pray for the people of Taif.

13. An Extraordinary Experience

At this bitter moment, when the Quraysh seemed to be on the verge of crushing Islam, the Prophet Muhammad had an extraordinary experience. He was lifted up to the heavens, and brought into the Presence of Allah. It was another turning point in his own life, and in the progress of Islam.

This experience of the Divine presence is important for us: though we may never have the good fortune to experience God with our whole being, both spiritual and physical, as the Prophet did, the inward, spiritual aspects of the experience can still be striven for and shared by every Muslim who is God-fearing and good.

It was during this experience, known as al-Isra and al-Mi'raj (The Night Journey and the Ascent), that Allah's commandment on prayer was revealed to the Prophet Muhammad. He reported that God wanted men to pray fifty times a day, but that on Moses' advice, he had appealed for a less difficult routine. At last Allah resolved that

THE ISRA AND MI'RAJ

One night as the Prophet Muhammad ﷺ slept next to the Kabah, in the same spot where Abd al-Muttalib used to sleep, the Archangel Gabriel woke him, and took him on a strange, white winged animal, called Buraq (lightning), from Makkah to the al-Aqsa mosque in far away Jerusalem. There the Prophet Muhammad met Abraham, Moses and Jesus and the other prophets, and they prayed together.

Then Gabriel took the Prophet through Heaven's gates, where he saw countless angels. One was Malik the Keeper of Hell, who never smiles. Malik, gave the Prophet a glimpse into Hell to let him see the misery of those who suffered there. The angels then took the Prophet through the Seven Heavens, one by one.

Beyond the Seventh Heaven, the Prophet passed through the veils covering that which is hidden, until at last he came into the Divine Light of Allah's Presence. The Prophet looked upon that which the eyes cannot see and minds cannot imagine, the Creator of the heavens and the earth.

Time, thought and feelings were suspended. The Prophet was aware only of great peace and the brilliance of pure light.

Too soon, the experience ended and he was brought back to earth. The Prophet was amazed to find the spot where he had lain was still warm, and the cup he had tipped over was still emptying. This incredible experience had taken place in less than a moment!

The next morning, the Prophet told the Quraysh what had happened. They didn't believe him. Many Muslims were amazed and wanted the Prophet to explain how such a thing could happen. But the Prophet's description of Jerusalem, and the caravans he had seen on the way back to Makkah, convinced them he was telling the truth.

For the Prophet, the Night Journey and the Ascent was a turning point. After years of persecution and the terrible sadness of losing both Khadijah and Abu Talib, the experience gave him great comfort and the strength to go on. He became convinced that God was always with him.

there should be five prayers a day. That has remained Muslim practice ever since.

This and all of the other important events in the Prophet's life, along with his observations and words of wisdom, were recorded by his Companions with great faithfulness and precision. These records came to

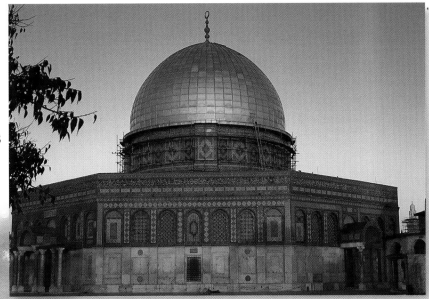

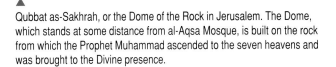
Qubbat as-Sakhrah, or the Dome of the Rock in Jerusalem. The Dome, which stands at some distance from al-Aqsa Mosque, is built on the rock from which the Prophet Muhammad ascended to the seven heavens and was brought to the Divine presence.

be known as the Hadith (traditions or sayings of the Prophet), and served as an ideal guide to righteous living. One collector of Hadith stands out from the others because of his learning and dedication. He was a cousin of the Prophet, by the name of 'Abdullah ibn 'Abbas. He was only thirteen when the Prophet died. It is said that he memorized no less than 1660 sayings of the Prophet, and would go to as many as thirty Companions to make sure that his version of each *hadith* was correct. Once when he went to a Companion to check on a *hadith* previously unknown to him, he found that he was having his afternoon siesta. Not wishing to disturb him, he waited outside in the heat and dust. When the Companion came out, he said: 'O cousin of the Prophet! What is the matter with you? If you had sent for me, I would have come to you."

"I am the one who should come to you," replied 'Abdullah, "for knowledge is sought—it does not just come."

14. The Migration to Madinah

▲
The Cave of Thawr outside Makkah, where the Prophet and his Companion, Abu Bakr, took shelter during his migration. The Quran says: When these two were hiding in the cave, he (Muhammad) said to his companion: Do not despair, Allah is with us. (9:40)

The Prophet's message was spreading far and wide and his following was growing. No longer all alone and easy to attack, the Prophet became the target of a murder plot hatched by the Quraysh, who wanted to stamp out Islam. In the meantime, the Lord commanded him to leave Makkah and go to Yathrib (now known as Madinah), to which many Companions had already migrated, and where he would be offered protection.

Under cover of darkness, the Prophet Muhammad and Abu Bakr slipped away on camel-back, leaving 'Ali Ibn Abi Talib lying in the Prophet's bed, so that the Quraysh would not realize he had left Makkah. When the Quraysh came to know, they offered a large reward for the capture of the Prophet and sent out search parties.

Guessing that the Prophet intended to go to Yathrib, (about 250 miles north of Makkah),

most of the search parties headed in that direction. But the Prophet and Abu Bakr went south, having arranged that a shepherd would cover their tracks with his flock of sheep. They decided to hide in the Cave of Thawr, just outside Makkah, until the search parties had given up.

On their third day in this cave, the Prophet and Abu Bakr heard the flapping of wings, and the sounds of men's voices and footsteps approaching. "If any one of them looks at his feet he will find us," whispered Abu Bakr. "No," said the Prophet, "We are not two but three, for, do you not know, God is with us. He will surely protect us." When the search party came to the entrance of the cave, Abu Bakr and the Prophet could

THE SPIRIT OF MIGRATION

Hijrah—migration—is never for gain, but for the higher purpose of serving Allah. The first great example was the Prophet's move from Makkah to Madinah, where the Muslims were now able to establish an important Islamic centre, and carry out the work of *da'wah* much more successfully than in Makkah. After the death of the Prophet, inspired by his well-known "Final Sermon", preached at the Mount of Mercy at Arafat to many thousands of people, most of the Companions and many others, migrated, and wherever they went, they engaged in *da'wah* work. Under their influence, whole societies, whole nations changed their faith, their culture and even their languages.

With the end of Muslim rule in Spain, the Muslims, to escape oppression, fled to the nearby lands across the Mediterranean. This stepped up the process of *da'wah* and led to the Islamization of North Africa. On the Indian subcontinent too, many migrant Muslims from Arabia, Iran, Afghanistan, etc., carried on *da'wah* work, so that now almost half of the total world Muslim population lives on the subcontinent. It was this Hijrah of the Companions after the Prophet's death which helped to create the vast Islamic domain, now commonly referred to as the Arab world. There are now more than one billion Muslims spread across the globe.

hear them talking quite clearly. Someone called out, "Forget it. There's no one in there." Then the footsteps were heard receding. The danger had passed!

After some time, the Prophet and Abu Bakr looked out from the entrance of the cave, where they were amazed to see that a spider had spun a web across its opening and a dove had made a nest just to one side of it. It was she who had flapped her wings at the approach of the search party. How could anyone have suspected that two men were hiding inside, when a delicate web covered the entry and a dove nested peacefully there?

Somewhat later, when they felt it to be safe, the Prophet and Abu Bakr continued on their journey to Yathrib. Because they took a long, winding route, and travelled only under cover of darkness, their dangerous and difficult journey took seven days.

▲
The Quba Mosque in Madinah, the first mosque to be built in Islam. The Quran called it, a place of worship which was founded upon piety from the very first day...wherein are men who love to purify themselves. Allah loves the purifiers. (9:108)

15. A New Beginning

▲ A minaret of the Prophet's Mosque in Madinah seen at sunrise.

man called Ayub al-Ansari. He became the Proph[et's] host. "Where shall I build a mosque? And how [big] should it be?" the Prophet wondered. His camel moved off, stopped, turned and walked back. "Th[is] is the place and the size of the mosque that Allah wishes us to build," said the Prophet. The land belonged to two orphans. "Take it," they said. Bu[t] the Prophet, being a m[an] of great probity, said[,] "No, I must buy it[.]" And he bought th[e] land from them[.]

It was now 622 A.D., twelve years after the beginning of the revelation of the Quran. As the Prophet, on his she-camel Qaswa, and Abu Bakr rode through the date groves and orchards outside Madinah, people gathered to greet them. On their entering the city gates, the welcome was joyous. All those who migrated with the Prophet were called Muhajir and were treated as brothers and sisters by the Muslims of Madinah, the Ansar. The Ansar even shared their possessions and properties with the Muhajir. From that day on, the town of Yathrib was known as *Madinat al-Nabi,* or The City of the Prophet. When the Prophet entered Madinah, every citizen wanted him to be his guest. "I shall stay wherever Allah wants me to," he said. "I shall stay in the house before which my camel stops." The she-camel, Qaswa, stopped in front of the house of a

WITH THE PROPHET IN MADINAH

The Prophet's journey from Makkah to Madinah—the Hijrah, or migration—was the first real step in the world-wide spread of Islam. That is why Muslims begin their calendar from the year of the Hijrah, 622 A.D. The Prophet Muhammad ☙, now a spiritual leader, brought to Madinah a new just social order with the mosque as its base. There, the first Constitution and the first Charter of Human Rights in the history of Islam were worked out and written down. With freedom of conscience and worship guaranteed to all—to rich and poor, to humble and highly placed, to Muslims and non-Muslims alike, Islam's vision of peace among peoples of all races and religions began to take shape. In Madinah, the Prophet built in his own courtyard the first mosque, or meeting place of the faithful, now known as al-Masjid an-Nabawi, or the Mosque of the Prophet. This became the centre of his activities from which he preached the message of Islam and where he had each new revelation memorized and written down by his Companions. Here too the third and fourth pillars of Islam were decided upon: alms-giving (*zakat*) and fasting (*sawm*). Everything, including our wealth belongs to God, the Prophet taught, and to purify our wealth and keep ourselves from greed, we must regularly give a portion of it to the poor and needy. This is not the same as the charity or generosity expected of Muslims at all times, but a specific annual duty to be performed by those who are wealthy enough. To do less would mean that love of things came before the love of God. To teach his followers self-discipline, and to recall for believers the month in which the first verses of the Quran were revealed, the Prophet Muhammad ☙ organized regular fasting in Madinah during the 29 to 30 days of the month of Ramadan.

Self-Sacrifice

After the emigration, the Muslims who came to Madinah from Makkah were clearly going to become a burden upon the local Muslims. The emigrants were empty-handed, while the local people (*Ansār*) had houses, lands, orchards, etc. But the Madinan Muslims, gave a hearty welcome to these newcomers. As the Quran says: "Those, before them, who had homes in the City (Madinah) and embraced the Faith before them, love those who have sought refuge with them; they do not covet what they are given, but rather prefer them above themselves, though they are in want. Those that preserve themselves from their own greed shall surely prosper." (59:9)

This willingness to make sacrifices is a great human quality. A daily necessity, it can mean withdrawing into the background so that others may go forward; suffering oneself to be able to give comfort to others; cutting down on one's own expenses so as to help others; suppressing one's own personality so that others may shine, remaining silent to allow others to speak; keeping one's vehicle to one side so that others may go ahead. Such self-sacrifice is called *isār*. It means putting others before the self. According to the Quran, it is those who possess this quality who will prosper.

16. The Peace Treaty

But the Prophet's departure to Madinah, instead of satisfying the Quraysh, made them much angrier. They now saw that the Muslims were all gathering in one place, and becoming stronger in the process. Only two years after the Prophet's migration, a one thousand strong army of the Quraysh approached Madinah to attack. The Quraysh camped at Badr, a group of wells about eighty miles from Madinah. Here they met the Prophet with a small band of believers. By divine help, the Muslims succeeded against heavy odds in defeating the Quraysh. The fighting lasted only a few hours, with very few of the Muslims having been wounded. Their defeat further enraged the Quraysh, and they launched more battles within the space of a few years.

The battle of Uhud took place in 624 AD, when the Makkans, under Abu Sufyan, attacked with about 3000 well equipped men. The Prophet's men numbered only 700. Up till then in all battles, the Arabs had always carried away all the booty which they could lay their hands on. But this time the Prophet gave strict instructions. No one was to take anything. They were not fighting for gain.

The battle raged furiously. The Quraysh women sang songs to encourage their men. If the Madinites had obeyed the Prophet, they would have won, but they broke their lines and started grabbing the spoils. Khalid ibn al-Walid, one of the Makkans, took advantage of this to lead his men through the Madinite ranks, killing them mercilessly. The Prophet himself was wounded on the head and lost two teeth when he was hit by a stone. He sank down bleeding. The Madinites thought he was dead and were disheartened. Then 'Ali, the Prophet's son-in-law, sprang forward, and a cry was heard, "The Prophet is alive!" The Madinites rallied together. At last the Makkans rode away. They had lost 14 men, while the Madinites had lost 70, among them the Prophet's uncle Hamzah. The Prophet was sad for his dead Companions, and, bowing his head in prayer, begged Allah to

forgive his men for their disobedience.

In 627 AD the Makkans attacked again. This time the Prophet was advised by a wise Persian called Salman al-Farsi to dig a trench around Madinah. Three thousand men dug for 20 days—the Prophet with them—and at last the trench was ready.

The Makkan army—24,000 strong—then arrived, but could not cross the trench. So they besieged the city. A whole month passed, but they found they still could not crush the Madinites. Then, suddenly, there was a terrible storm and the wind raced furiously, blowing away their tents and stores. The Makkans decided to retreat and left quickly for their own city. So ended the Battle of the Trench.

The Cave at the foot of Mount Uhud outside Madinah, where the Prophet Muhammad was taken when he was wounded.

"A Clear Victory"

In the sixth year of the Hijrah, the Prophet, acting on the word of God, set out on a pilgrimage to Makkah along with 1400 Companions. But the Quraysh stopped them at a place called al-Hudaybiyyah, some eleven kilometres from Makkah. Here the Prophet signed a peace treaty with the Quraysh, which was called by the Quran "a clear victory." This provided for ten years of peace between the Quraysh and the Muslims. There was to be no war or treachery between them. The Treaty was concluded with the agreement that the Muslims would not make the pilgrimage that year, but that the following year the Prophet Muhammad ﷺ and his followers would be free to go to Makkah and stay for three days.

The Terms of the Hudaybiyyah Peace-Treaty were as follows:

1. that the Muslims would return to Madinah that year without performing the 'Umrah;
2. that the pagans would, however, allow them to do so the next year, provided their stay in Makkah did not exceed three days;
3. that Muslims would not bring any arms with them;
4. that no Muslim residing in Makkah would migrate to Madinah, but if any migrant in Madinah wished to return to Makkah, he would not be prevented;
5. that pagans visiting Madinah would be permitted to return to Makkah but Muslims visiting Makkah would not be allowed to return;
6. that tribes were at liberty to join any of the two contracting parties.

17. Inviting to Islam

The Treaty of Hudaybiyyah was a great victory, because it gave the Prophet Muhammad ﷺ time to turn his attention to the other tribes of Arabia and the Kings and Emperors of the countries bordering Arabia, to tell them the message of Islam. With the treaty, the Muslims were also able to return to Makkah for the pilgrimage, and though they could stay only three days, they made a deep impression on the people of Makkah, who saw the simplicity and devotion of their lives, the kindness and respect with which they treated each other, and the love they had for their leader, the Prophet Muhammad. Within just two years, the number of people siding with the Prophet ﷺ had risen from 1500 to 10,000, including several leading men of Makkah.

The Quraysh were again furious, and regretted having signed the Treaty of Hudaybiyyah. But if they broke the Treaty openly, they would clearly look like villains, so they began breaking it secretly, by supplying weapons on the quiet to the Muslims' enemies. Aware of this betrayal, the Prophet knew that he must take over Makkah.

The Prophet Muhammad wanted to avoid bloodshed, so he did not tell any of his followers of his plans to capture Makkah. He gathered the biggest possible army — ten thousand in all — for he aimed at frightening the Makkans into submission, so that the city could be captured without any need for

fighting. When they reached the outskirts of Makkah, the Prophet ordered them to spread out and told each man to light a fire. The sight of so many fires in the night would persuade the Makkans that they were surrounded by a huge army and that it was useless to try to fight. In fact, seeing them, and hearing the report of the Muslims' readiness from one Makkan scout, one of the Quraysh exclaimed, "Who has the power to confront them?"

Indeed, no one did. The capture of Makkah was, as the Prophet had planned, a totally bloodless victory.

The Mosque of the Prophet at Madinah. The mosque and its surrounding plazas can hold over a million worshippers at a time.

Letters of the Prophet

After the peace treaty of al-Hudaybiyyah, the Prophet Muhammad sent letters to neighbouring kings.

These letters, short and simply written, gave the basic message of Islam. Here is the letter which the Prophet wrote to Khusru, the King of Persia:

"In the name of Allah, the Merciful, the Beneficent. From Muhammad, Allah's messenger, to Khusru, the leader of Persia. Peace be to him who follows right guidance, believes in Allah and His messenger, and declares that there is no deity save Allah, the only God, Who has no partners, and that Muhammad is His servant and messenger. I wish to convey to you Allah's call, for I am Allah's messenger to all mankind, sent with the task of warning all those who are alive that doom will befall on those who reject the truth. If you submit to Allah, you will be safe. If you refuse, you shall bear the responsibility for the Magians (i.e. your people)."

18. A Forgiving Conqueror

Victors are usually proud and happy to take revenge on their victims, but not the Prophet Muhammad. After his conquest of Makkah the Prophet displayed the utmost humility. When he entered Makkah, his head was bowed so low that people could see his beard touching the camel's saddle. Standing at the door of the Kabah, the Prophet delivered an address: "There is none worthy of being served save the One, Allah. He has fulfilled His promise and offered help to His servants. He alone has brought the hosts of enemies low."

The Prophet did not claim any credit for the victory: he said it was entirely Allah's doing. And he went on to forgive the Quraysh:

"I say to you as Yusuf (Joseph) said to his brothers: Let no reproach be upon you this day. Go, you are free."

Even Uthman ibn Talhah who had once refused the Prophet's entry to the Kabah and persecuted him, was later given back the key to the shrine, and it remains with his family to this day.

Then the Prophet Muhammad turned to the Kabah and pointed to the idols that had been placed there. He recited from the Quran:

The Door of the Kabah, screened by a thick curtain made of mixed cotton and silk on which passages from the Quran are inscribed in fine calligraphy worked in golden thread.

▶

"In the Name of Allah, the Beneficent, the Merciful... Truth has come and falsehood has vanished away. Lo! Falsehood is ever bound to vanish."

All of the idols crashed to the floor. The Prophet and his followers then cleaned and purified the Kabah, and Bilal, who had a strong and beautiful voice, was ordered to climb to its top and give the call to prayer.

The Kabah, the House of Allah, was at last restored to the purpose for which it

had been built thousands of years before by the Prophet Abraham as a safe, holy place for the worship of Allah, our Creator. To this day Makkah remains the spiritual centre of Islam.

The Prophet returned to Madinah, and the Quraysh became Muslim, and one by one, the rest of the tribes in Arabia declared their faith. As each tribe joined Islam, the Prophet sent people acting on his behalf to teach them about Islam, which seemed new to them, but which was actually the completion of the Prophetic tradition beginning with Adam and continued by Noah, Abraham, Moses and Jesus, upon all of whom be peace. The Prophet himself continued teaching, guiding and conveying Allah's instructions to his followers.

But even though he commanded wide power and authority, the Prophet Muhammad remained a humble and ordinary man. He was the ruler of Arabia, but he wore no crown and did not sit on a throne.

19. A Simple Man

Despite his position as leader, the Prophet Muhammad ﷺ never behaved as if he was greater or better than other people. He never made people feel small, unwanted or embarrassed. He urged his followers to live kindly and humbly, releasing slaves whenever they could and giving in charity, especially to very poor people, orphans and prisoners, without any thought of reward.

The Prophet himself was never greedy. He ate very little and only simple foods. He preferred never to fill his stomach. Sometimes, for days on end, he would eat nothing but raw food. He slept on a very simple mattress on the floor and had almost nothing in the way of home comforts or decorations. One day Hafsah, his wife, tried to make him more comfortable at night by folding his reed mat double—without telling him—to make it softer

▲ The seven mosques complex in Madinah an example of simple architecture during the early days of Islam.

for him. That night he slept peacefully, but he overslept and missed the pre-dawn prayers. He was so distressed when he found out that he never slept like that again.

Simple living and contentment were the key teachings in the Prophet's life: "When you see a person who has been given more money

and beauty than you, look then to those who have been given less." In so doing, we will thank God for His blessings, rather than feel deprived.

People used to ask his wife, 'Aishah, the daughter of his first and most loyal Companion Abu Bakr, how he lived at home. "Like an ordinary man," she would answer. "He would sweep the house, stitch his own clothes, mend his own sandals, water the camels, milk the goats, help the servants at their work, and eat his meals with them; and he would go to fetch what we needed from the market." He seldom had more than one set of clothes, which he washed himself.

He was a home-loving, peace-loving human being. "When you enter a house, ask God to bless it," he would say. He greeted others with the phase: "As-salamu alaykum"—which means: "May peace be upon you,"—for peace is the most wonderful thing on earth. He was a firm believer in good manners, always greeting

Truth and Paradise

Once a man came to the Prophet and said: "O Prophet, by God, it is my earnest desire to go to heaven. Tell me what I should do for this to happen." The Prophet replied, "Speak the truth." When man speaks the truth he does good deeds. His heart is lit up with the light of faith, and when the heart is blessed with the wealth of faith, he can be sure of an entrance to God's paradise.

— *Nuqush-e-Seerat*
by Hakim Muhammad Sayeed

people kindly, and showing respect to elders. He once said: "The dearest of you to me are those who have good manners."

All his recorded words and actions reveal him as a man of great gentleness, kindness, humility, good humour and excellent common sense, who had a great love for animals and for all people, especially his family. Above all, he was a man who practised what he preached. His life, both private and public, was a perfect model for his followers.

The Prophet did not have many children. His two sons by Khadijah died when they were very small, and another baby boy, whom he had later on, also died. However, he had four daughters, all of whom married and had children. Of them, the most famous, was his youngest daughter, Fatimah, who married his nephew 'Ali and gave him two grandsons, Hasan and Husayn, and two grand daughters, Zaynab and Umm Kulthum.

20. Prayers of the Prophet

The Prophet Muhammad taught us that prayer is a way of saying how we need God's grace for every single thing we have, and how God's power over all things is total. There are different kinds of prayers. Some are to praise Allah for all the wonderful things in the world and some are to thank Him for His blessings. We often ask Allah to forgive us, telling Him of our fears and worries. At other times we pray for others to be helped and cared for.

The Prophet advised people to pray in times of peace and plenty, and not just in times of difficulty. One of his favourite prayers in the Quran was for parents: "My Lord, have mercy on them, as they have raised me up when I was little." He also said brotherly love was a great virtue. In his prayers to his Creator for all of humanity, he would say: "O Lord, all Your servants are brothers."

The Prophet urged his followers to ask Allah for forgiveness: "Allah holds out His hand at night for those who have done wrong during the day to repent. And He holds out His hand during the day for those who have done wrong at night to repent."

To have God's special protection, he would pray, "Allah, save me from leprosy, insanity and incurable diseases. O Allah, save me from want, poverty and being humbled. Save me from doing wrong or being wronged."

The Prophet forbade believers to pray for their own deaths or even to think about suicide. "If anyone is in a very dreadful state," said the Prophet, "let him pray, 'O Allah, keep me alive so long as life is good for me, and take away my soul to Yourself when death is best for me.' "

One who prays for another in his or her absence will most probably have his prayers fulfilled for, as the Prophet explained, to every believer God has assigned an angel who says,

"Amen! And to you the same." His own selflessness is shown by his praying even for those who harmed him.

The Prophet, a keen observer of nature, regarded all natural things with a great sense of wonder. For example, seeing a new moon, he would pray, "O Allah, let its rays bring us security, peace and submission." Speaking to the moon, he would continue, "My Lord and Your Lord is Allah. May this be a crescent of guidance and goodness."

▲
The Mosque of the Two Qiblas, or Masjid al-Qiblatayn, in Madinah. Here the Prophet Muhammad, while leading the faithful in prayer, was asked in a revelation of the Quran to turn towards the Kabah in Makkah instead of Jerusalem, which was the earlier qibla.

The Prophet would urge people to remember Allah constantly, as he believed that "one who remembers his Lord and one who does not remember his Lord are as unlike as the living and the dead." Therefore, the Prophet would urge his followers to remember God by day and by night, even if only by saying a few words. To make it easy for them to do this, he taught them a short prayer, saying:

Two phrases are light on the tongue
yet heavy in the Balance
and beloved by the Merciful:
*Subhan Allah wa bihamdihi,
Subhan Allahil-Azeem.*
(Glory be to God and all Praises are His, Glory be to God, the Magnificent.)

21. The Prophet's Hajj

Once more, in the tenth year of the Hijrah, the Prophet Muhammad set out for Makkah to perform his Hajj. This time about 100,000 believers accompanied him. This pilgrimage is commonly known as the Hajj of the Farewell (*Hajjat al-Wida*). Here he explained the rules of Hajj, and gave his famous speech, known as the Final Sermon (*Khutbah* of the *Hajjat al-Wida*).

Upon reaching Makkah, the Prophet and his followers put on the white, seamless sheets that showed their equality before Allah. This is called *ihram*. Then the pilgrims went directly to the Kabah and walked round it seven times in a counter-clockwise direction. This is called the *tawaf*. As pilgrims arrived they called out:

> Here I am, O Allah,
> here I am!
> Here I am,
> O You without equal,
> Here I am!
> Yours is the kingdom,
> the praise and the glory,
> O You without equal,
> God Alone!

This is the prayer called the *talbiyah*, which is the answer to the divine call to come and give one's life wholly to Allah.

Next, they ran back and forth seven times between the small hills of Safa and Marwah in memory of the time when God tested the Prophet Ibrahim ﷺ and his family. This is called the *sa'i*, and it shows the soul's determined search for that which gives true life. According to the Quran, God had told Ibrahim ﷺ to leave his wife, Hagar, and their son Ismail (or Ishmael) in His care in the uninhabited valley of Makkah. In the barren desert the two soon began to die of thirst. Frantic, Hagar ran back and forth between the hilltops, trying to spot a passing caravan in the distance. But there was none. Finally, when all seemed lost, a spring gushed

forth at the feet of the suffering child, Ismail. This spring is now known as the Zamzam well. It reminds pilgrims of the truth that when all hope is gone, God remains to give healing strength and life to the soul.

Now the pilgrims had completed the rites in the Sacred Mosque in Makkah. On the eighth day of the Hajj, the pilgrims went to the valley of Mina, about ten kilometres from the Kabah, where God had tested Ibrahim ☪ by ordering him to sacrifice his son, Ismail. At the last moment, God stopped Ibrahim, and sent a ram to be sacrificed instead.

▲ The Sacred Mosque now encompasses fully 356,000 square meters (88 acres), including the rooftop prayer areas and the open plazas surrounding the mosque. It comfortably holds a million worshippers, but during Hajj and Ramadan more than twice as many crowd into it and fill its adjoining plazas.

Our Lives Should Revolve Around the Lord

5000 years ago, the Prophet Ibrahim ☪ was commanded by Allah to lay the foundations of the Kabah—the House of God in Makkah—and to call people to make a pilgrimage (Hajj) to it. People throughout the ages have responded to this call, and now every year over two million people come from every corner of the globe to perform this rite.

Hajj is one of the five tenets of Islam, and every Muslim, having the means, and healthy enough to travel, must go on this pilgrimage once in his or her lifetime. All pilgrims have to wear special, very simple clothes so that all may appear equal.

The Sacred Mosque at Makkah, once quite small, is now huge enough to hold as many as one million pilgrims at a time. All the pilgrims go round the Kabah seven times, to show how man's life must revolve around God. Then they carry out other rites such as running between the hills of Safa and Marwah, stoning the pillars of Satan at Mina, and standing before their Maker on the Plain of Arafat, praying and listening to sermons. The Hajj ends with a final encircling of the Kabah.

22. The Last Sermon

On the ninth day, the pilgrims proceeded to the Plain of Arafat to stand on the Mount of Mercy. There they stood in the sweltering heat, bare-headed, and thought about God and prayed for His mercy. This is called the *wuquf*. Here, during the sermon on that day of the Prophet's Hajj, the last passage of the Quran was revealed to the Prophet Muhammad: "Today I have perfected your religion and I have completed My blessing upon you, and I have approved Islam for your religion."

After praying, the Prophet spoke to his followers. He told the Muslims to let the Quran and his own example be their guides in life. He ordered them to stop living as they had done before Islam. Revenge, a very old tradition in Arabia, and usury were to be ended. Property was to be respected. And, he said, "Know that every Muslim is a Muslim's brother." This was a new idea to the quarreling tribes. "Have I made myself very clear?" asked the Prophet after every point.

After the sermon, the Prophet looked up and cried: "My Lord! Have I delivered aright the Message I was charged with and fulfilled my calling?"

Then he asked the gathering: "You will be asked about me, so what will you say?"

They answered with one voice: "We bear witness that you have conveyed God's message and have performed your duty and that you have meant goodness for us." Pointing his index finger toward heaven and then to the people, he said: "Oh, Allah, be witness; O Allah, be witness; O Allah, be witness."

Ramadan with the Prophet

The Prophet said: " Those who fast are destined to have two joys: One at the time of *iftar* and the other when they meet their Lord."

The observance of fasting (which means no eating and drinking from dawn to sunset) during the 29 or 30 days of Ramadan, the ninth month of the Islamic lunar calendar, is one of the five pillars of Islam. It is a crash course in self-discipline, making us more aware of the necessity to do good and avoid evil, and more thankful to God for His grace and compassion. Believers during that period spend longer than usual on their prayers and the recitation of the Quran, and give more in alms. They also avoid lying, cheating, obstructing justice or oppressing their fellow men. Such selfless behaviour is required of believers, not only during Ramadan, but throughout their entire lives. Every believer, man and woman— must observe the fast. But those who are ill during Ramadan, or too elderly, or on a journey, may feed the poor instead, or make up the days of fasting later on. The fast is not meant to cause any undue hardship.

The Prophet ended his speech by saying, "Let those present convey the message to the absent." By sunset, they headed back toward Mina, gathering pebbles along the way. On the next day, they performed the ritual of casting their pebbles at Satan, symbolised by three pillars set up in memory of how Abraham and his family resisted the temptation of Satan. In doing this, the pilgrims pledged themselves once more to Allah and promised to do their best to drive any devils out of themselves.

Finally, an animal was sacrificed, and the pilgrims returned to perform the farewell *tawaf* of the Kabah. The meat from the sacrifice was

The pilgrims standing on the slopes of the mountain of Mercy at Arafat. This being one of the most important rites of Hajj, the Prophet said, Arafat is Hajj.

sent to the poor and needy.

Three months after returning from the Farewell Pilgrimage to Madinah, the Prophet fell ill. The Messenger of God died on 8 June 632 A.D. He was 63 years old. As the news of his death spread, people refused to believe it. 'Umar ibn al-Khattab, with his sword unsheathed, swore that he would slay anybody who said that the Prophet had passed away. Seeing the chaos, Abu Bakr mounted the pulpit and announced: "O people! For those who worshipped Muhammad, Muhammad is dead. But whosoever worshipped Allah, let him know that Allah is alive, and will never die."

These brief words sum up an important belief Muslims have about the Prophet Muhammad ﷺ. Muslims do not worship any human being. They worship God and God only.

23. Exemplary Character

An old hand-written copy of the Quran in Kufic script.

book of Islam — the Quran — was revealed in the 7th century A.D. by the Archangel Gabriel.

Events do not unfold in it in the order in which they happened —as they would in a long story or novel. Its text, with its 6,236 verses divided up into 114 chapters, is more like great rhythmic passages of prose, set to wonderful music, which conveys with total clarity all that was revealed of God's will to the Prophet fourteen hundred years ago.

Young Muslims start reciting the Quran from a very early age, and many go on to memorize the whole text. The Quran is the only book in the history of mankind which is

The Prophet Muhammad is thought of as the noble prophet and a perfect man, whose way of life and character are an example to everyone. He is also regarded as the perfect ruler and statesman. The Muslim community he created at Madinah is the example which all Muslim communities should strive to be like. He serves as a model for millions of Muslims. They try to copy the minute details of his life, such as the way he worshipped, washed, dressed and ate. For Muslims the Prophet Muhammad ﷺ had "the most excellent character" and of him the Quran says, "Lo, God and His angels shower blessings on the Prophet. O you who believe! Ask blessings on him and salute him with a worthy salutation." The Prophet Muhammad ﷺ was buried in the mosque in Madinah that he himself had helped to build. Today, millions of Muslims visit his tomb and pay their respects to one of the great prophets of Allah.

It was to this exemplary person, the Prophet Muhammad ﷺ, that the great, holy memorized from cover to cover. Today, there are thousands and thousands of people in the world—they are called *huffaz* (sing. *hafiz*)—who know the entire Quran by heart.

By the time of the Prophet's death, many thousands of men and women knew the Quran by heart, and the whole text also existed in written form. Abu Bakr, the Prophet's closest Companion and the first Caliph of Islam, saw the need to preserve the Quran, not just in human memory, but in a single authentic text. So he had the Prophet's chief scribe, Zayd ibn Thabit, and other scribes and memorizers put down the revelations in writing. Later, the third Caliph, Uthman ibn Affan, had six official copies made of Abu Bakr's final text, which were then sent to the Muslim provinces. Till today, the Quran has remained absolutely unchanged.

The Quran—The Book of Allah

Being the true word of Allah in human language, the Quran is the eternal book of instruction for the whole of mankind. It provides correct and understandable answers to all the questions which arise in an inquisitive mind, such as, "Why has Allah placed humanity on earth?" "What is His scheme of things in creating such a vast universe?" "How should we lead our lives?" "What will happen to us after death?" And so on.

After having memorized all of the revelations which the angel Gabriel brought to him, the Prophet instructed his Companions to memorize them too. He also called for a scribe to dictate each one back to him. There were about twenty nine scribes, the more important of whom were Zayed ibn Thabit, Ali ibn Abi Talib, Abu Bakr, Umar, Uthman, Abdullah ibn Sa'd and Mu'awiya ibn Abi Sufyan. Thus the entire Quran was written down and memorized by hundreds of Companions in the lifetime of the Prophet. The Prophet also recited the entire Quran twice in front of the angel Gabriel, thus putting its surahs in the correct order. Shortly after the Prophet's death, the Quran was put together in the form of a book (or *mushaf*) by the first Caliph Abu Bakr and, during the time of the Caliph Uthman, several copies of it were made and sent off to various countries. Till today two such copies exist in museums in Istanbul and Tashkent.

From the time of the Prophet Muhammad, when the Quran was revealed and written down on the leaves of date-palms, parchments, etc., the script of the Quran has gone through a number of stages. Most of the early copies of the Quran were written in a script with square-shaped letters known as Kufic. In the early tenth century, Ibn Muqla, who was considered the father of Arabic calligraphy, developed its rules and defined the shape, size, curvature and position of each letter. Later on, other scripts such as Thulth, Naskh, Muhaqqaq, Rayhani, Tauqi and Riqa were developed. Thus the Arabic script continued to change and rise to new heights. Today it is a form of the Maghribi style of script, which was developed during the period of the Ottoman Caliphs of Turkey, which is mostly used to transcribe the Quranic text.

To introduce Islam to the neighbouring lands, the Prophet Muhammad sent out letters containing verses of the Quran through his Companions to various rulers. These letters were first translated into the local languages before presenting them to the respective Kings. Thus the first translations of portions of the Quran were done during the Prophet's own lifetime. Later on, the Quran was translated in parts into Persian and during the tenth century, the Quran was printed by wooden blocks. The first translation of the Quran into Latin was done in 1143 and published in 1543. A German translation was published in 1647 and the first English translation appeared in 1648. Over the years, the Quran was translated into several major and regional languages and today there are about 500 complete translations of the Quran in English.

In addition to every Muslim man, woman and child having to study the Quran and follow it, the giving of its message to non-Muslims is also a duty. In his last sermon, the Prophet Muhammad urged his followers to convey the message of the Quran "even if only by a single *ayah*."

24. The Angel and the Three Men

Once the Prophet Muhammad told his Companions the story of three of the Children of Israel—a leper, a bald man and a blind man. To test the gratitude of these three poor men, Allah sent an angel to each of them.

To the leper, the angel said, "Of all things, which would you most love to have?" The leper replied, "A beautiful complexion, beautiful skin and a cure for the ailment for which people shun me." So the angel passed his hands over the man, and his wishes were granted. The angel again asked, "Of all things, what would you most love to possess?" "Camels," he replied. So he was given a pregnant she-camel. As the angel left, he said, "May God bless it."

To the man with the diseased scalp, the angel said, "Of all things, what would you most love to have?" The man replied, "Beautiful hair and a cure for the disease for which people shun me." So the angel passed his hands over him and his wishes were granted. Again the angel asked, "Of all things, what would you most love to possess?" "Cows," he replied. So he was given a pregnant cow. And the angel said, "May God bless it."

To the blind man, the angel said, "Of all things, what would you most love to have?" He replied, "My sight restored by God, so that I can see people." So the angel passed his hands over him, and he regained his sight. Then the angel said, "Of all things, what would you most love to possess?" "Sheep," he replied. So he was given a ewe with its lambs. And the angel said, " May God bless them."

All the animals multiplied, so that the first man had a valley full of camels, the second valley full of cows and the third a valley full of sheep.

Later, the angel came in the guise of a leper to the first man and said, "I am a poor man, unable to travel any further without God's help—or yours. By the One who has given you wealth and a beautiful skin and complexion, give me a camel to ride on my journey." The man replied, "I have too many obligations." The angel said, "I seem to recognize you. Weren't you once a leper whom people shunned? And weren't you poor before God gave you so much?" The man replied, "I inherited this wealth from a nobleman, who inherited it from a nobleman." The angel said, "If you are a liar, may God turn you back into a leper."

Then, in the guise of a bald man, he came to the man who had once had a diseased scalp and made the same request as he had to the first man. His plea was similarly turned down. The angel said, "If you are a liar, may God turn you back into a bald man."

Coming to the third man in the guise of a blind man, he said, "I am a poor, homeless man, unable to reach my destination, unless God, or you, can help me. By the One who restored your sight, give me a ewe to help me on my way." The man said, "I was blind, and God restored my sight. So take whatever you will and leave whatever you will, for, by God, I will not grudge you anything you take for His sake." The angel said, "Keep your wealth, for you were only being tested. You may keep your blessings, but your companions have lost all."

Many Kinds of Charity

The Prophet said, "Give alms from the right hand, but your left hand should not come to know of it." But over and above giving alms and feeding the poor, the Prophet gave much wider meaning to the concept of charity, as he believed that every good act was a form of charity: smiling at a fellow human being; showing the road to a person who has lost his way; removing hindrances such as thorns and stones from the road; assisting the blind; helping a person to mount his beast; uttering pure, comforting words and replying to questions with mildness. All of these for the Prophet were forms of charity.

25. And the Stone Moved

The Prophet Muhammad ﷺ once told a story of how three men, out for a walk in the mountains, were caught in a rainstorm. They quickly took shelter in a cave, but the entrance to it was at once blocked by a huge stone which came hurtling down the mountain side. Now it was impossible for them to come out. So they began to pray to God, recalling the good deeds they had done, in the hopes that Allah would be pleased with them and set them free.

The first one said that he and his wife and children were living with his aged parents. Whenever he returned with his herd, he milked the animals and then offered the milk first to his parents and then to his children. One day, he went far away and, by the time he came back home, it was very late and his parents had fallen asleep. He milked the herd as usual and brought the milk to his parents, but seeing that they were sound asleep, he did not feel like wakening them up. His children ran to him for their milk, but he felt it was not right to give it to them before he gave it to his parents. So he stood there all night, waiting for his parents to get up. They did not waken till the break of dawn. Only then, when they had had their milk, did he give any to his children.

What he did that day had been done to please God, and he begged his

Maker, if He had seen any virtue in his behaviour, to set them free. Miraculously, the stone moved a little bit, but not enough to let them come out.

The second man said that he had a cousin with whom he was very much in love and whom he was very keen to marry. But she refused to marry him and stayed away from him. Then a time came when she was in dire need of help, because of a famine that year. She came to him and he gave her 120 gold coins. Then he wanted to marry her forcibly, but she pleaded with him not to do so. He agreed to her request and, turning away from her, he allowed her to go away and take the gold coins with her. The man begged God to remember that he had done this out of fear for Him, and beseeched Him to help them. So the stone moved another little bit, but the gap was still not wide enough for them to come out of the cave.

The third man said that once he had hired the services of a workman for a bushel of rice. When the work was completed, he gave the man his bushel of rice, but the workman, not liking the quality of it, went off without it. So he kept re-planting it until he had earned enough money from its sale to buy some cows. Years later, the workman returned and demanded his wages. He told the man to take away the cows which had greatly multiplied by that time. And this he promptly did without leaving a single cow for their owner. After telling this tale, he begged God to release them, as he had done this good deed for fear of Him. So the stone moved a little more and made a big enough gap for them to come out of the cave.

26. The Message of Peace

The Prophet's most important task was to bring peace to the world. To this end, he urged people to accept the fact that, regardless of skin, colour, language, lifestyle or dwelling place, they were all blood brothers and sisters. Only if they saw each other in this light could there be mutual love and respect.. To his followers he would say, "You are all Adam's children, and Adam was made of clay," and, asking them to live in peace, would add , "A true believer is one with whom others feel secure — one who returns love for hatred." He taught believers that returning love only when love was given was base human conduct. The true believer caused no harm to those who mistreated him, but chose rather to work for their good. The Prophet himself led the way with his common sense, kindness, gentleness, humility, and good humour. He greatly loved all people and even animals.

The Prophet was a leader, yet, believing he was no greater or better than others, he never made people feel small, unwanted or embarrassed. He urged his followers to behave kindly and humbly, to release slaves whenever possible and to give alms, especially to very poor people, orphans and prisoners — with no thought of reward.

He was the soul of goodness, so that even if people harmed him, he would pray for them, remaining unruffled, no matter how badly he was treated.

The Hadith—
Sayings of the Prophet

The Hadith, i.e. the sayings and deeds of the Prophet, form a Muslim code of conduct second only to the Quran in religious importance. Handed down from person to person, starting with the Prophet's Companions and contemporaries, the truth of their content ("*matn*") was guaranteed by the narrators' reliability. This system was called "*isnad*".

The best of the six well-established books of Hadith (*al-kutub as-sittah*) are the "*Sahih*" ("The Authentic") of al-Bukhari and Muslim.. The others are by Abu Dawud, al-Tirmidhi. Al-Nas'ai and Ibn Majah. Other famous works include the *Muwatta* of *Malik* ibn Anas, the *Masnad* of Ibn Hanbal and the *Forty Hadith* of Nawawi.

In setting this example, he encouraged people to turn to God, as a Being of surpassing greatness. He wanted all men and women to be unworldly and to have such great peace of mind that nothing could disturb them. Then, with no grudges to bear, they would seek no revenge, but would merely turn all events, whether material or spiritual, into food for thought.

Throughout the first thirteen years of his prophethood, the Prophet Muhammad preached in Makkah, although the

An inside view of the Prophet s Mosque in Madinah.

Makkans bitterly opposed this. When things became impossible, he left for Madinah. Wars were waged against him, but he convinced his enemies that peace had greater power than war, as was shown by the peace treaty of Hudaybiyyah. In this the Prophet agreed to every demand of his enemies, on the assurance that, in return, peace would necessarily ensue.

His life went through various stages of well-being and extreme hardship, yet never once did he stray from the path of moderation. At all times, and right till the end, he remained the patient and grateful servant of the Almighty, bringing his message of peace and tolerance to all mankind.

27. Glossary

Akhirah The Hereafter, life after death, when each person will be called to account for his or her deeds.

Ansar The Helpers, those people of Madinah who helped the Prophet Muhammad ﷺ and his Companions when they migrated to their city from Makkah.

Al-Kutub al-Sittah The six well established books of Hadith. These include collections of al-Bukhari, Muslim, Abu Dawud, al-Tirmidhi, al-Nas'ai and ibn Majah.

Dhul-Hijjah The month of the Hajj, the last month of the Islamic calendar.

Dawah The introduction of Islam to non-Muslims.

Hadith Sayings or traditions of the Prophet Muhammad ﷺ. These are an important source of Islamic law.

Hafiz Plural, *huffaz*, someone who knows the entire Quran by heart.

Hajj The annual pilgrimage to Makkah. (One of the five pillars of Islam).

Hijrah Migration. This refers to the migration of the Prophet Muhammad ﷺ from Makkah to Madinah in June 622 A.D. It marks the beginning of the Islamic calendar.

Hilf al-Fudul A group of Makkans formed to help weak and deprived people. In his youth, the Prophet Muhammad ﷺ was an active member of this group.

Ihram The state that pilgrims must be in to perform Hajj. Also the name of the two white, unsewn, plain cloths worn by male pilgrims to show equality and purity.

Isar Self-sacrifice, the willingness to make sacrifices for others. The conduct of the Ansar of Madinah was a shining example of this great human quality.

Isra The night journey of the Prophet Muhammad ﷺ from Makkah to Jerusalem. See MI'RAJ.

Jahiliyyah Days of Ignorance, the period in Arabia before the coming of Islam.

Jibril The angel Gabriel, who delivered Allah's messages to the Prophet Muhammad ﷺ.

Kabah A cube-shaped building that stands in the centre of the grand mosque in Makkah towards which Muslims face while praying. It was originally built by the Prophets Ibrahim and Ismail (peace be upon them).

Lailatul Qadr The Night of Power, when the very first revelation of the Quran was made to the Prophet Muhammad ﷺ.

Mi'raj The ascent through the heavens of the Prophet Muhammad ﷺ.

Muhajir The migrants, those who migrated to Madinah from Makkah along with the Prophet Muhammad ﷺ.

Muslim One who submits himself to Allah by following the religion of Islam.

Niyyah Declaration of intention. Islam teaches that intention has a great place in a believer's life, as the Prophet Muhammad ﷺ said, "Deeds will be judged according to intentions."

Nabi A person chosen by Allah to bring His message to humanity. The Prophet Muhammad ﷺ was the last of the Prophets.

Quran The Divine Book, revealed to the Prophet Muhammad ﷺ as the final revelation of Allah to mankind.

Riba Usury, the charging of interest on a loan, which is forbidden in Islam.

Salah The five daily prayers observed by Muslims, as a form of worship of Allah. (One of the five pillars of Islam)

Sawm Fasting in the month of Ramadan (One of the five pillars of Islam).

Shariah The eternal ethical and moral codes of Islam based on the Quran and the Sunnah.

Sirah Biographical writings about the conduct and examples of the Prophet Muhammad ﷺ.

Sunnah Literally, path or example. It applies particularly to the example of the Prophet Muhammad ﷺ and includes what he said, did and approved of.

Sahabah Singular *sahib; sahabi*. Companions. The term is used for those who were closest to the Prophet, kept frequent company with him, memorized the Quran, assimilated his teachings and transmitted his sayings. However, in general, anyone who believed in the Prophet Muhammad's mission and had seen him once in his life time is regarded as a Companion.

Tafsir Commentary and explanatory notes on the Quran.

Talbiyah The invocation the pilgrim often repeats after putting on *ihram* during Hajj.

Taqwa Piety, to be prudent and conscious of Allah. That is, being careful not to overstep the limits set by the Almighty.

Tawaf Going around the Kabah seven times in an anti-clockwise direction, having the Kabah on the left hand side.

Tawhid Belief in the Oneness of God—the most fundamental of Islamic concepts.

Umrah The lesser pilgrimage to Makkah, which may be performed at any time of the year.

Wudu The washing of hands, face and feet before prayers.

Wuquf Literally, "standing." Staying in the Arafat valley and especially praying there in the standing position on the second day of Hajj.

Zakat Purifying tax on wealth. It is considered as a religious duty and a social obligation (one of the five pillars of Islam).

ﷺ *Sallallahu alayhi wasallam*. May the peace and blessings of Allah be upon him. These words are said every time the Prophet Muhammad ﷺ is mentioned, as a mark of respect and salutation.

﷐ *Alayhis Salam*. Peace be upon him. These words are said every time the name of a prophet is mentioned, as a mark of respect and salutation.

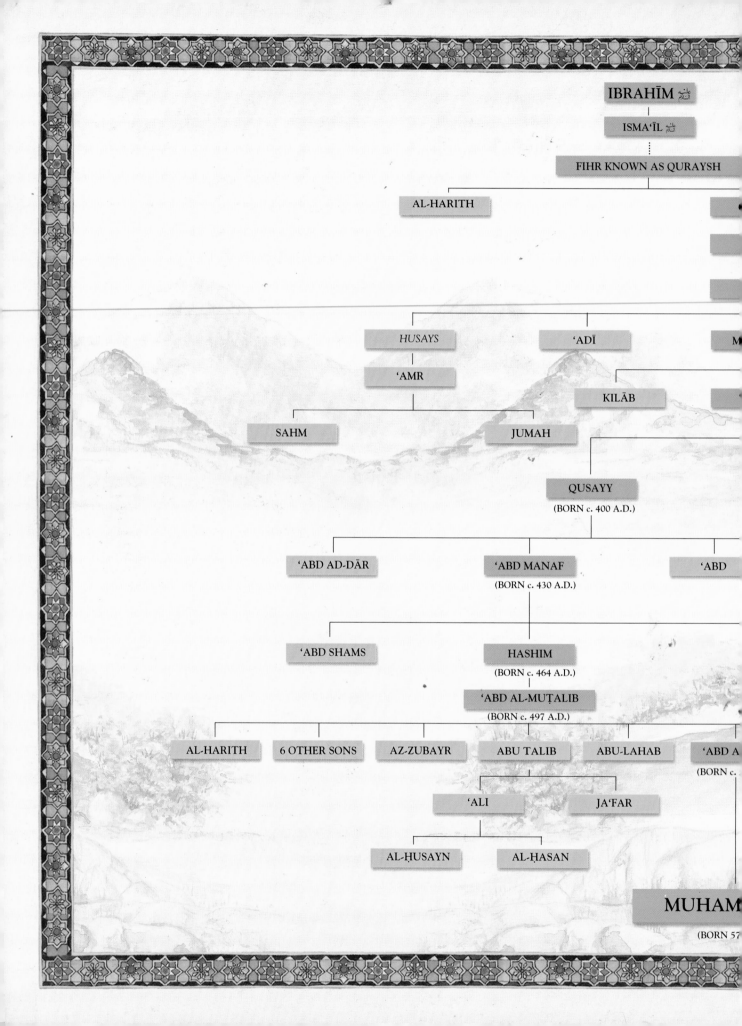

IBRAHĪM ﷺ

ISMA'ĪL ﷺ

FIHR KNOWN AS QURAYSH

AL-HARITH

HUSAYS

'ADĪ

M

'AMR

KILĀB

SAHM

JUMAH

QUSAYY
(BORN c. 400 A.D.)

'ABD AD-DĀR

'ABD MANAF
(BORN c. 430 A.D.)

'ABD

'ABD SHAMS

HASHIM
(BORN c. 464 A.D.)

'ABD AL-MUṬALIB
(BORN c. 497 A.D.)

AL-HARITH

6 OTHER SONS

AZ-ZUBAYR

ABU TALIB

ABU-LAHAB

'ABD A
(BORN c.

'ALI

JA'FAR

AL-ḤUSAYN

AL-ḤASAN

MUHAM

(BORN 57